WORDS YOU WILL NEVER READ

poems by jessica katoff

WORDS YOU WILL NEVER READ
BY JESSICA KATOFF

ISBN-10: 0-9903180-6-0
ISBN-13: 978-0-9903180-6-4
First Print Edition, 2017

10 9 8 7 6 5 4 3 2 1

Author: Jessica Katoff
Editor: Kat Savage, William C. Hannan
Cover Design: Jessica Katoff

DEDICATION

Wholly, undoubtedly, and eternally for my father.

FOREWORD

Grief does a lot of interesting things to a person. When I sat down to write this book, it was mere months after I lost my father—my biggest champion and my first love. As I sat with the pages, I thought this would be a book of sadness, of guilt, of pain, of shame. But, as I started to write, that's not what came out. Again, grief does a lot of interesting things to a person. I found myself relishing in the good that followed the hurt, in the kindnesses afforded to me, in the healing. I found myself able to feel things beyond the pain. And that's where this book came from. Some of the pain still made it into these pages, but this is not about my father. It is about everything I have experienced since I lost him. This is a book about surviving and all that comes with that—how he taught me to be strong enough to stare down any heartbreak and carry on. And though my father will never read these words, I'm sure he knows that I am okay now, that I have grown from this. And you, you who will read this book, I hope you learn something. I hope you are tender with yourself when you are hurting. I hope you can find joys and victories in every tragedy you endure. I hope you heal when you're ready. I hope this book helps you do so. It certainly helped me.

synonyms for
HEARTACHE

Until you feel it,

until the ache
makes its way
beneath
your skin
and sinks in,

grows there,

thrives there,

you will never
understand.

I pray,
down to
my bones,
you never do.

It's tricky,
the way muscles
remember things.

How
eight of them
still part my lips
to ask you about
the most
trivial of things.

How
twenty-nine
still move my hand
to dial your number
in the middle
of the day.

How
the one
deep in my chest
still beats,

even though
you are gone.

I was not
ready.

I had not
yet
learned
how to
hold things.

You were
already
in pieces.

Please
do not
fear
the dark;

there is
so much
of it
in me.

It's harder now,

to let you
hold me,

now that you
have seen
the things
I have
defeated,

now that you
hold me

like a weapon.

So many
parts of me
died

every time you
buried yourself
inside me,

not like a lover,

but like a grave.

I don't know
how long it will take
for the wounds
to close and fade,
to become vague
memories
of this pain.

I don't know
why I cannot stop
tearing them open
just to pass the time.

I know what happens
when we unbolt this door,
and leave this room.

It all gets
left behind.

The way I drank you in,
and all the confessions
made against my thighs.

And maybe that's
for the best.

We can't make
all-consuming love
all the time.

There would be
nothing
to leave behind.

I carry you

in my chest.

One
deep,
deep,
deep
breath.

And I know,

if I cannot
let you go,

you will be
my death.

I hope
you will
haunt me

forever.

If this is how
I must
have you,

please stay.

All the others
were just
somewhere
to rest my hands
while they waited
for you.

And I am sorry
I was impatient.
I did not wait
for yours to be
the only skin
they knew.

I did not think
you would be here,
in my hands,
so soon.

There was
something
about the way
you looked at me
that first time,

and I knew

you would
never truly
see me
at all.

We live
here now,

in this
silence,

the way
we once
made homes
inside of
each other.

You told me
I was
too delicate
a flower,

then brought
fistfuls
of me
to your
new lover.

It is useless
to wonder;

the what ifs,

they are
just as
intangible
as you
have become.

All of
those hands
close enough
to touch you

that aren't
touching you

should feel
ashamed.

I was
nothing more
than a highway
to you,

something
to be used;

you were
always only
passing through.

I kissed
another

and tasted
betrayal

for the
first time;

my mouth
has always
been yours,

even if yours
has never
been mine.

I came
to you
in winter,

my branches
bare

in apology,

and still,

you would not
warm me.

Tell me you
feel nothing.
Admit it,
finally and forever,
and I will let myself
burn
one last time,
down to embers,
to ashes,
to nothing;
this torch
is heavy,
and I am tired
of carrying it
for someone
who will not
hold me.

The price
you paid
for this love
was far
too much;

the price
I now pay
for letting you
will never be
enough.

I crave you
like six feet deep
does company;

I swear,
this wanting
will be
the death of me.

I often wonder
which words
your tongue
wraps around
to describe me
now.

I am sure
they are not
the same ones
you once
whispered
into my mouth.

It's intimate,

this sadness,

how it holds me
closer than
you ever did.

This morning,
I watched
as the sun
made its way
into our bed,
and kissed you
in ways
I know
I never will
again.

For
too long,
I confused
use
for
need.

You
reached
for me.

You
did not
ache
for me.

Tell me,
was it on
the first night
that you felt it
the way I did?

Or did I
grow on you
over time,
the way
you faded
for me?

Most days,
I find it hard
to hold myself
together;

most days,
I find it hard
to believe
you are
holding
someone
else.

It was never
your mouth
that told me
you loved me.

It was
your hands,
three in the morning,
white knuckled
and gripping mine
on the bathroom floor.

It was Sundays,
slow and simple,
driving through
red clay,
and the way I would
feel your glance.

It was how you
pressed against me,
my arms on the glass
of that hotel window
as the sun went down.

It was one million
small things
that alone
said nothing at all.

So forgive me
for not being able
to believe you
when your mouth,
your beautiful mouth,
tells me it's done.

We want
for it.

We wait
for it.

The end
that never
comes.

Damned
to be
eternal,

apart
from
each other.

You would
probably
taste like
forgiveness
by now,
but I still
can't swallow
all the wrong
I have done.

It took me
all of these years
to understand
that sometimes,

just sometimes,

leaving
is how
some people
love.

I speak
of you in
the past tense
now;

it is the
saddest sound
to ever leave
my mouth.

definitions for LOVE

Please,
be patient
with me.

I have been
seed, soil, and sun
for too long.

No one has
tried to
help me
bloom
before now.

Maybe none of this
will mean
a goddamn thing
by the time
we're through,
but my god,
right now
in this bed,
feeling nothing
with you
means
everything.

I want you
to beg,

just once,
for me;

let me
know,

just once,
for me,

that what
I want
is what
you need.

Even a breath
between us
is too far now.

I fear the day
when no distance
will be far enough.

It will always
come back to the way
you kissed me,
your lips
a quiet surrender,
and there was never
a sweeter victory
than the taste of you
defeating your fears.

I am a
beautifully
bound
collection
of sorrows,

pages
and pages
of pain,

and
somehow,
you read on,
always eager
to witness
what comes
next.

I know you will
chew me up
and spit me out,
but I cannot resist
crawling inside
your mouth.

This is the
preamble.

This is
before.

I have
barely
touched you,

and you
are already
trembling.

Here.

Here is
where it
starts.

With you.

You,
in my
bed.

And me.

Me,
all over
you.

This.
This is
the place
where
need
is born,
and will
not end.

No amount
of longing
or aching
will bridge
this divide;

that is
something
only our
bodies
can do.

When did it
become
this?

My lungs
not knowing
how to work
without
your lips
pulling the air
from them.

My skin
not feeling
like my own
unless it is
rubbing up
against yours.

Why
am I
more you
now
than I am
myself?

You have
explored

the unkempt
and unsafe,
the untraveled
and unknown

parts of me,

and still,
you press on,

mouthfuls of
my marshes,
handfuls of
my hillsides,

intent on not
getting lost in me

this time.

For so long,
I wore
shadows
as shields;

your light
crossed
every single
battle line.

Let me
pretend

the stars
are alive,

and they are
watching us,

just for tonight;

we are too
beautiful
like this,

bare
beneath
them,

to go
unseen.

Your hands
met my skin,
soft and reverent,

but all I wanted
was for you to
claw your way
right through me.

You are
the burning building
I will always
run into,
because we are
conditioned
to try to save
the things
we love.

Tonight,
I don't want you
to touch me.

I just want to
exist with you.

Breathe
beside you.

Just be.

We are captives
of these bodies,

that's true,

but only
for now.

Never mind
your skin.

Set me free
in the parts
of you
that matter.

Familiar,
but so
foreign,

you are
everything
I never knew
I wanted.

All these souls,

in all these
bodies,

across all this
space,

over all these
lifetimes,

and there
you were,

finally.

Open palms.

Open mouth.

I will always be
an open invitation

for you,

whenever
you will
have me.

If this is
how it
ends,

soft,
quiet,
still,

with
your hand
in mine,

it would
all be
worth it.

One moment,
that's all
it was,
your time
away
from me.

Years,
but just
a moment.

And that's
okay.

We have
epochs
ahead of us.

Every now and then,
I remember
what it was like
to love you,
in a different time,
when we were
in different bodies;

I hope
in some other
lifetime,
with different marrow
in our bones,
we are able to
again.

My hands
will always
reach for yours,
even now,

especially now

that you have
filled yours
with another.

Think of me
as sunlight.

Let me kiss
your face.

Imagine
I am
there.

metaphors for STRENGTH

In all
of her
phases,

the moon
is still
whole

behind
her
darkness.

I am
the same.

There is
no magic
in this
sadness.

That
comes
after.

The magic
is in
the survival.

Reach
inside
yourself.

Be gentle
with even
your most
unsightly
of parts.

Do not
pull them
like weeds.

They will
flower,
if they are
well-tended.

There are
wars
in you.

I know.

There are
armies
in me.

Let me
fight.

It is my hope
that one day
I will be
strong enough
to carry all of this
longing,
to avoid
growing weak
at the sight of
every stranger
who offers
to let me
rest it
in their bed.

I have wondered
what it would be like
to have you

close,

closer,

impossibly close,

so close
you are
burrowed
beneath my skin,

and I take a step back.

I laid down
my arms
in the arms
of another,

and I finally
understood

love

should not
look like

war.

I will
never know
how you
reached past
all of the pain
in me,

and still
pulled me
close.

I find you
in the most
unexpected
of places.

Mostly,
I find you
staring back
at me
when
I lose sight
of myself.

I will not
give you
soft.

I will not
give you
tender.

I will not
give you
ease.

But I will
give you
poetry,
and to me,
that is more.

There are
parts of me
that need you.

You will
know them
as the
parts of me

that push you
away.

Some people
will be
bridges,

others
may be
roads;

take them
where you
must,

but know they
will never be
your home.

I have found
hopelessness
in more places
than I can count,

in the bottoms
of bottles
and tucked into
empty beds,

but I have
never
found it
in you.

For ages,
there was

nothing,

and then
there was you,

and nothing

could stop us
from becoming

everything.

Allow yourself
to feel fear.

Allow yourself
to conquer it.

Allow yourself
the spoils
of that war.

Where
it hurts
in you,

those spaces
pain carved
out of you,

those are
the parts
of you

where
I belong.

I will still be
every star
in the sky

for you,

even if
you never
glance up.

I am sure
there are
scraps of me
hidden
away,

in the
farthest
corners
of you,

lingering,
and alone,

even now,

ages since
you were
last inside
of me.

I have
finally
let myself
forget
the things
you did
to me.

This is not
forgiveness.

This is only
survival.

If you miss me,
do not call me
at night,
with that
half handle
of whiskey
tucked in
beside you.

Do it in
the morning.

Tell me the way
you reach for me
in the sobering light,
that you are drunk
on the sadness
of your empty hands.

You will not
win me back
in the dark.

I have come
too far.

Let go
when you
are ready,

not when
they pull
away;

there will still be
pieces of them
in your palms
worth clinging to

for a while.

I will look back
on our time
and see
so many things,
but I promise,
I will never
look for
the sorrow.

There will always
be people
whose hearts
you cannot crack;

keep yours
open to them
anyway.

I may have
my father's
blood
on my hands,

but it is still
in my veins;

I was born
for this fight.

Let yourself
fall apart.

People
still worship
ruins,
you know.

Not all things
that grow
in you
will be
beautiful.

There
will be
vines,
weeds,
thorns.

Let yourself
still cradle them
like they are
sunflowers.

There will
be moments
when the pain
will almost
feel safe.

Let yourself
feel that.

Let yourself
feel whatever
you need to.

But know
you will
feel better,

in time.

If nothing else,
I hope I have
brought you
some measure
of comfort
in your darkest
of times;

you have
brought
miles in mine.

I have worried
whether or not
my roots
were rotten
from the start,

but here I am,

thriving
in a place where
everything else
has died.

I press
my hands
against
the darkness,

aching for
a fight.

It surrenders
to me now.

I write
these words
you will
never read,
because
they are
the only way
you remain;

I give them
away to anyone
who will
read them,
because
I need to
let you go.

ABOUT THE AUTHOR

Jessica Katoff is a marketing professional by day and a fiction novelist and contemporary poet by night. A southern Florida native, she currently lives on the outskirts of Atlanta, Georgia with her two very fluffy pooches. This is her fourth poetry collection.

Want to know more?
Visit jessicakatoff.com or connect with Jessica on:

Facebook | facebook.com/jessicakatoff
Instagram | instagram.com/jessicakatoff
Twitter | twitter.com/jessicakatoff

She also accepts love letters at jessicakatoff@gmail.com

Made in the USA
Columbia, SC
13 September 2017